MY PAPER DREAMS

SELECTED POEMS

SHAHAB MOGHARABIN

Translated from Persian by

FATEMEH LILAZI
&
ALIREZA ABIZ

Published by Unsolicited Press
www.unsolicitedpress.com

For information, contact the publisher at
info@unsolicitedpress.com

Editor: S.R. Stewart
Cover Designer: Mark Rodart
Production Editor: Eric Grant

Unsolicited Press Books are distributed to the trade by Ingram.
Printed in the United States of America.
ISBN: 978—1—947021—42—6

I owe a singular gratitude to Ms. Fatemeh Lilazi and Mr. Alireza Abiz who translated the poems in this book and put them within reach of a wider range of readers.

I express my deepest thanks to S. R. Stewart for putting great effort into editing the final copy and thus giving the book a much better and presentable form.

I would also like to thank Mr. Ahmad Pouri, a prominent poetry translator, for his invaluable suggestions for the translation of the poems.

CONTENTS

FROM

WORDS AS MINUTES

A desire to lose myself

A desire to lose myself
is growing inside me,
a desire to go missing
somewhere in a virgin land,
a desire to become lost
in deep remote thoughts.

I am tired of feeling tired,
of sitting here and talking of sitting here
and of the feeling that wears me out.

Thoughts of breaking free do not release me,
the thought of freedom in departure.

In the depths of a journey,
I want to travel with the rains,
camp above the seas,
swim through the sands.

I want to break free from air
to join the vacuum of love
which fills me to the brim,
which lifts me up off the land and off the air
and scatters me around
where everything has been set free.

It takes me to the place and the time
when beauty may find me again.

A desire to go missing
is growing inside me.

A crow is sitting on a wooden bench

A crow is sitting on a wooden bench in the park.
A fragile cane appears behind a window,
slowly approaches the wooden bench in the park.

The eyes are blank
only a twisted gaze like knotty wood.

Behind the vacant window on the staircase's shoulder
no sign of a feminine beauty has been seen for a very long time.

In the darkest of nights,
only the steps' echoes can be heard
returning from the park.

I set off down the road I loved

I set off down the road I loved
and it took me
where I didn't love.

When you let go of all

When you let go of all
and befriend the countryside roads
and speak to the trees lining on both sides,
When the forthcoming turn becomes a question
and the valley turns into the response,
what do you think you would see
except a descending cloud?

And where do you think the country roads will take you
if not to that eternal little room
which takes you to sleep
behind windows smeared by dried raindrops?

Even dreams grow old

Even dreams grow old
yet continue to move forward,
drag themselves beside me
whose hands I've been holding on to.

Which one of us will collapse sooner,
dreams that view me as a shadow
or me who take them for real?

BY THE SIDE OF THE PURPLE ROAD, I SAW MY CHILDHOOD

A heavy snow fell

A heavy snow fell;
One tree turned pretty,
One tree broke apart.

Sometimes the rain takes his colorful violin

Sometimes the rain takes his colorful violin
to play for the sun
and the sun holds up her skirt and dances
showing off her bare knees.

Sometimes the tree turns so green
you fly in ecstasy—
At times it looks so disheveled
you swirl around like a leaf
and fall down.

Sometimes a cuckoo cries for something that doesn't exist.
At times under a safe soffit
it guards something in such a deep silence
as if it is all that there is.

Sometimes a star sends you a bit of joy
with a blink from afar.
At times the moon goes hiding
and takes your joy away.

Sometimes in a breeze everything goes away.
At times in a shadow everything remains.

Everyday they take me

Everyday they take me
from one room to another.

How could I escape?

Hanging from the branch
the memory of swing is turning before my eyes.

How can one hang himself
with a rope that does not exist
or put a car into neutral and drive downhill
into a valley that does not exist?

The walls take me everyday
from one prison to another.

A moment approaches gently

A moment approaches gently
and whispers secret words.

It wakes you up even if you were asleep.
It finds you even if you have already left,
and whispers secret words.

Thereafter
disappears again gently.

I will throw myself into a river

I will throw myself into a river,
not into the one that pours into a lagoon
where a few birds are hanging around—
but what do they know about freedom?

I will throw myself into a river,
not into the one that pours into a sea;
Seas do not appreciate silence.

I will throw myself into a river,
into the one that flows to the place
where all those drowned were taken.

I had forgotten the park

I had forgotten the park
and the bench
where I had left my hat.

The smell of decaying leaves woke me up.
I went back to that fall afternoon fifteen years ago.

Falling on the bench
leaves were whirling down.

I couldn't find my hat,
but there she was again
smiling.

This time
I could make up for that missed opportunity.
This time I could.

Moss was floating on the pond water.

Walls of sand

Walls of sand,
hands moving between them like crabs,
windows of matchboxes,
that little room leaf—carpeted by wind;

This is the same house my father built years ago
and I destroyed it with my baby hands.

This is the same house I have built for you anew
with my manly hands.

There is only one difference:
There used to be a river here carrying away our tears
but today
the wind has taken away all the memories.

No one knows where this road leads

No one knows where this road leads.

Mysterious shadows emerge and disappear
and the smiling face behind the almond blossoms
breezes in and out between the branches.

I left behind the almond blossoms and the smile hiding behind
to be traveling on this train
which came all the way to here.

And then

And then
the silence behind the trees carried on
and then
the empty pool reflected children's screams
and then
an afternoon which was long gone

The statue by the pool watched
and the autumn like that elapsed afternoon
was going away and coming back.

The street vendor had nothing to sell
except the air of burst balloons.

And then
the wind passed through the tree branches and shouted:
Call again!

And then
the elapsed afternoon came back.

And then
the water fountains washed the eyes of the statue again
and the balloons were filled with the autumn air,
red and yellow.

And then
the silence behind the trees receded.
Children came back from garrisons,
burst the balloons one by one

and went back to their barracks.

And then
the afternoon elapsed.

And then
the silence behind the trees went on.

Snow covered your footprints

Snow covered your footprints.
Earth covered your laughs.

Snow has melted.
Floods have turned the earth upside down.
But there is nothing on the horizon,
except a thin blade of grass
playing in the breeze.

A dragonfly

A dragonfly
with its clear wings and timorous eyes
sitting on trembling paper in my hand
has turned into a poem.
What should I do to make it stay?

Should I insert a pin in its back
to darken its wings and its eyes
leaving nothing
but the corpse of a poem on the paper?

Or should I let it fly
and leave this blank page
dead in its silence?

We won't go beyond that line on the horizon

We won't go beyond that line on the horizon
and it doesn't make much difference be it far or close.

What I want is to lie on the wings of a bird
which flies a high dream on the azure bed,
a dream
that I will never admit was a dream.

FROM

WIND WILL LEAF THROUGH THIS BOOK

In all stations

In all stations,
you are standing
waving at me.

I alight frantically
in all stations.

But you are gone—

Let our date be right here

Let our date be right here beside this headstone
when I am not here anymore.

I will be back after we are gone
and this early autumn breeze which comforts our cheeks
will show up
and will testify to my return.

You will not see my broken face.
The breeze will enable us to kiss
and will caress us.

So uncanny they are, those teashops on the roads
where strangers cause such a commotion,
but sometimes one must stay on the side of a remote road
under a dusty pomegranate tree
and watch from outside
how the early autumn wind blows
and carries our faces away.

Such a pity we did not hold hands.
We knew we had to let go.
We knew that this absurd whirling wind will scatter us away.

Why did we fail to hold hands?

You will not see my broken face again
but the wind will bring my cheek close to yours
and will caress you.

Like the hands of a clock

Like the hands of a clock
windmills turn in the wind.
They turn and crush everything
like the hands of a clock.

The new meetings

The new meetings brought along many distances
and some strangers we have yet to name.

Our children are made of different memories,
and we,
not so old to confuse each other's tone of voice,
not so young to re—live our sweet dreams,
are blamed for breaking an old pledge,
a pledge we think we had never made.

However,
we remember well the narrow path we covered
from mother's home to this broad junction,
and we remember we had never purchased any tickets
to bring us to this station,
and we never expected these unfamiliar faces
who are here not to welcome us
but to escort us to the final station.

But still
we have not grown so dumb to have forgotten our childhood
and not to recognize
—among all these children
who are wandering in streets and squares—
those who may not be made of our own memories
yet are determined to visualize our long and lofty dreams.

The house still stands

The house still stands
but its inhabitants are dead.

Or maybe
the house has been destroyed
though the inhabitants are still there.

No,
the house still stands,
inhabitants are alive,
but something seems to be missing.

I'm not sure.

Water carries away the leaves

Water carries away the leaves in the gutter—
Branches are looking for something in the wind.

The gray silence before the dawn

The gray silence before the dawn
is a dead rooster's crow.
Don't you hear it?

I wanted to change the world

I wanted to change the world.
It changed
but it wasn't what I worked for.

I wanted to change mankind.
It changed
but it wasn't what I wished for.

Now I just want to keep you,
hold you as you were with no change at all,
wrapped in the paper of my dreams.

You will never change.
You will remain as you were:
a river of fire.

Tomorrow is here standing before me

Tomorrow is here standing before me
asking me what I wanted.

I push him aside by my cane
gazing at the distance as before
waiting.

We fought against the clock's hands

We fought against the clock's hands
in a battle similar to Don Quixote
fighting the windmills.

They are ringing the church bells

They are ringing the church bells
in the silence between black garments and white flowers.

What I hear
is the endless sound of my school bells.

In advance

In advance we threw our gaze somewhere far,
far ahead.

Later we took to the road,
carried our steps limping along.

We reached our destination
but there was no eye left to see what we came to see.

My name is not Robinson Crusoe

My name is not Robinson Crusoe.
I am not a prisoner on an island.
My friends are countless,
more than all the seconds of all the days of all the weeks.
The cannibals' island is not on my horizon.

So why do I constantly plan to escape?
Why do I constantly fear the cannibals?

This world is also a painting

This world is also a painting—
You could erase the moon off the face of the sky,
leave the space blank.
You could draw the rain and let it fall,
if not with hands, you could use your eyes.

You could act the same as the hand
that keeps erasing our paintings
leaving their space blank
for all eternity.

We are old—time acquaintances

We are old—time acquaintances;
For years, we watched the moon set
and for centuries,
the moon watched our lives set.

The sky is blue

The sky is blue.
The spring is green.

How come my pencil writes in black?

The train left

The train left.
I fidget on a bench in the station,
not that I'm left behind,
I've spent years
waiting for the next train.

Love and hate

"Love and hate are two sides of the same coin,"
The woman said.

The man tossed the coin and asked,
"Love or hate?"

"Love,"
The woman said.

"You won,"
The man said and showed her the coin:
It was hate.

Man and woman were two faces of the same coin
constantly turning over
in the aura of love and hate.

A blade of grass

A blade of grass
next to another blade of grass
in a dense grassland

We bend in the wind
toward the other
and the other bends
toward the other
and the other
toward the other
and the other ...

WHISTLING IN THE DARK

I move the stool aside

I move the stool aside and put it by the window.
I am now friends with this stool
as I am with this rope hanging from the ceiling—
I pat it on the back and let it stay right here.
(Maybe another time!)

But now your sun is shining on me.
The anticipation has made my day beautiful.
The magic of your words keeps me enchanted.

I sit on the stool and smile like lunatics
staring at the rope swings.

It feels as if an old clock's pendulum
is counting my moments.

I wish I were a tree

I wish I were a tree
and knew the language of silence,
so I could comprehend you.

Not all roads

Not all roads
can be traveled by foot;
Let's hold hands.

Let's be deluded again

Let's be deluded again:
You believe my words
and I will believe your eyes.

What does the world have to offer us
if you take your eyes off me
and I stop telling "I love you"?

I wanted to keep this love a secret

I wanted to keep this love a secret.

All of a sudden I realized
all words knew my secret.

That's why whatever I write
turns into a love poem for you.

Our pomegranate tree

Our pomegranate tree
displays blossoms in the yard,
you are not here.

Should I smile
or should I shed tears?

How come

How come the tree branches are not swaying today?
What if it is a sign
that I don't love you anymore?

When I think of death

When I think of death
I know I should be thinking of life.

When I think of life
I know nothing else exists,
I should be only thinking of you.

When I think of you
I don't know what to do.

Let's build a home together

Let's build a home together
with no doors to the outside world,
only a small window
to sit and watch the street and laugh
at these wandering prisoners.

You are a flower

You are a flower.
Even a gentle breeze will disturb your peace.
You have now stepped into my heart
where an endless storm is raging.

What a story you are reading to me

What a story you are reading to me!
When you tell me about its end
my adventure just begins.

My youth was lost in your arms

My youth was lost in your arms.
Had you given me a moment
I would have found it.

You let me out of your arms—
Maybe you were right,
my days had passed.

Sooner or later
I bundle my regrets up
like a bouquet of flowers
and propose to the Lady of the Earth
who will not say No;
She will open her arms.
She will embrace me and all I have.

I will bestow her everything I have
with an eternal regret:
the loss of my mouth.

How can I still say I love you?

I am afraid of love

I am afraid of love.
Of love I am afraid.
All the love poems that I write
are a child's whistling in the dark.

I picked you out

I picked you out from among people's phrases.
You were a sweet word.

You were not 'love';
Love is bitter.
You were not 'friendship' or 'desire';
Friendship tastes dry and desire is hot.

You were sweet
like 'dream', like 'sleep'.

I picked you out from people's phrases,
embraced you in the brackets of my arms
like a beloved word.

You flew like 'sleep'
and were lost
among the voices.

Your lovers will not stay forever

Your lovers will not stay forever;
They will be gone, one by one.
They will disappear.
Every new kiss
shoots a bullet at the previous one.

One by one, they will leave.
Only one will stay, the strongest of all,
the one who wanders around you all the time.

Me?
No!
Your last bullet finished me off.

Only one will stay,
the one who is stronger than me.
He will sit face to face with you.
He will stare into your eyes
and there will be no escape from him.

I have known him for long;
Loneliness is the name.

I am light again

I am light again.

The wind restored the leaves on the branches.
They turned green and are gently moving
in the same wind that crushed them once.

I am green again
now that I have mastered my desire for you.
I am light
and back on my own branch.

The wind must blow the leaves away,
disturb them,
destroy them,
scatter them on earth,
but I have mastered my desire for you,
I am light
and back on my own branch.

I am happy.
I am calm,
yet I don't love life.

I don't know,
maybe I should go back into the wind
to find you again
somewhere, someday.

I was looking for two words

I was looking for two words
like two leaves whispering in each other's ears
or two lips humming in search for a kiss.

I was looking for two words
like a set of earrings for your ears.

In clusters, all words who loved your hand lined up
casting a band on your hand.

You latched onto them
tearing apart the string of words
dashing them all each to a corner.

I am looking for one word,
a silent word
which would amass all the words
on your lips
like a kiss.

A lightning in the sky

A lightning in the sky,
and immediately I fathom it all.

Recount it, I could not,
but in the language of this rain.

I stared into the end of the alley

I stared into the end of the alley of our regular date venue;
I saw the shadow of the tree
and a restless sparrow flutter.

I saw your image in the water

I saw your image in the water.
You left,
I began stalking the river.

Oh, lonesome moon

Oh, lonesome moon,
you have lost your other half!

Don't be impatient!
It will find you in a fortnight.
You will be a full moon again, but
my other half
will never come back.

No

No,
they are not made of paper
easily blown away by wind.
Take the paperweight you left on my dreams,
put it on the wind!
It is my dreams that have disconcerted the wind.

They say I am dangerous

They say I am dangerous.
Don't take it seriously.
This raised fist is just to show off.
I don't scream anymore.
I don't whisper anymore.
I just make funny faces
for the ghosts who come to visit.
They bring empty cans
and leave quickly,
their footsteps:
tick tock— tick tock— tick tock ...

To the hell with it!
When they leave, I laugh aloud.

But when you were gone, my sweetheart,
I wept quietly.
You knew I wasn't dangerous,
this raised fist is just to show off.
You should have taken these chains off.
I would then knock down these ghosts who come to visit:
tick tock— tick tock— tick tock ...

I was falling snow

I was falling snow;
I surrounded you,
embraced you,
caressed your cheeks,
kissed you on your shoulders,
and in tiny fragments,
fell under your feet.

You stepped on me;
I became firmer, harder, stronger.

You shone on me;
I melted away.

Perhaps for the rest of the day

Perhaps for the rest of the day
the phone keeps ringing
and no one picks it up.

Perhaps this cup of tea gets cold,
the wind smokes the rest of my cigarette,
the ashtray gets filled with a gray head.

Perhaps those who take me away would tell themselves:
"Poor man couldn't finish his poem."

But, I am more fortunate than this,
for me everything doesn't end here;
There are things beyond this poem,
and you will never forget
how much I have loved you.

You are my birth

You are my birth.

No wonder
the further I move forward,
the farther you get away from me.
You are the moment of my birth.

Othello

You are free Desdemona!
It is me who will never be free
from the chain of your hands.

Give me back my handkerchief,
I don't want you to see my tears.

Get up

Get up,
Let me show you a piece of shoreline
at the end of this cul—de—sac.

Where there is a shore,
surely there is a sea.

Believe me,
I can hear the waves.
Whatever else we saw was just a dream.

Get up, Let's go,
This is our own shore.
We will sail the sea from there.
We will do the impossible.
We will sleep together,
will quench the thirst of our fish
and will dream that
whatever we saw was just a dream.

Hurry up,
The sun is to set soon
and I fear that the dark waves
could take away our shore.

There was only one key to my home

There was only one key to my home;
I handed it to you,
and wandered the streets.

We were apart

We were apart,
far apart.
We could not hear one another.

We got close,
saw each other's lips moving,
could not hear the voice.

We got closer,
heard each other's voice,
could not understand the words.

We got closer,
understood each other's words,
could not taste them.

We got closer,
so close to have our lips locked
and our words twisted.

Twisted words cast us apart,
far apart.

You held me in your arms

You held me in your arms,
on the cross
which was my destiny.

We are two branches of the same tree

We are two branches of the same tree;
If only the wind blew from both sides!

It has been a while

It has been a while
since I've been tired of words.
They bash in groups,
sit inside my head
like a flock of birds on a tree.

I clap my hands loudly,
shouting out loud;
They fly away and scatter around.

But there is always a silent bird
who neither fears or flies away
nor sings her song.

The sea is deep

The sea is deep,
loneliness is deeper.

Give me your hand,
Let's hold on to one another
before we drown.

We follow each other

We follow each other
like two seasons;
Your storms sweep away my leaves,
My rains pour down on you.

We meet each other
like day and night
killing one another in our twilights.

We move together
like two seconds
running away from each other.

I will swim against the tide

I will swim against the tide
until the river changes its course,
or I drown
in the dream I had of you.

SOMEBODY KNOCKED AT THE DOOR

A knocking at the door

A knocking at the door!

She gets up,
fixes her hair,
opens the door.

Wind!

She comes back in
with disheveled hair.

Days go by

Days go by
and we linger on
leaning on the sunset.

She opened her umbrella

She opened her umbrella;
She was alone.

She closed the umbrella;
Together they left
with their cheeks wet.

The river flows

The river flows
and forgets the rock
which created its waterfall.

I stretch my hand

I stretch my hand.

What could I write
on the paper gone with the wind?

I'm back from the dead end

I'm back from the dead end to this open road,
wide open road.
Come and look!
It still doesn't lead anywhere.

I took off the mask I had on

I took off the mask I had on.

Behind the mask,
there is someone left
who doesn't see,
doesn't say,
doesn't know,
doesn't ask,
doesn't want.

Behind the mask,
there is someone left
who doesn't stay.

Sometimes we laugh

Sometimes we laugh,
sometimes we cry
under silent stars.

There are still many ways

There are still many ways
to make yourself laugh:

You could stand in front of the mirror
and make funny faces.
(This is funny only once.)

You could sit and recall all your life's follies
counting them one by one.
(This may bring many bitter laughs.)

Or if neither does you any good,
get up and burst into a fit of laughter
(Even hysterical laughter can solve a problem.
Let them call you mad
when madness is your only excuse for laughing.)

If none of the above worked,
clench your hands on the table,
rest your forehead on your fingers
and burst into tears,
cry until you run out of tears.
This will certainly open some space inside you
for a smile.

And then

And then
nameless grasses grow out of our hearts
with shadows which darken our names.

They blossom in the shape of our hearts.

A gentle breeze brings them close
whispering to each other.
Another breeze blows from the other side
and they forget it all.

On the way back

On the way back,
my eyes were fixed ahead
but searching for something behind.

I kept on going
but never arrived.
I kept on going
but I didn't know
if I was going back
or was going backward.

Our world is framed in a mirror

Our world is framed in a mirror
which gives a lone meaning to a thousand faces:
alone!

Walls are upright

Walls are upright.
Doors are devious;
they pull you in
and take you to the other side of the wall.

Walls drive you crazy.
Doors lead you astray.

A tree branch bends

A tree branch bends,
seeks its shadow.
The shadow is gone
under another branch.

Someone keeps knocking at the door

Someone keeps knocking at the door.

Here a dead man's dream lives
and dreams don't open the door for anyone.

Everything said was futile

Everything said was futile
and so was silence.
Words hid in silence
and silence hid in words.
It was not in vain that we kept our secret in our eyes
and closed our eyes on one another.

To pass through the night

To pass through the night
I had to say the password.
And the password was a long silence
lasting till morning.

How is the cradle restlessly rocking

How is the cradle restlessly rocking
able to calm you down?
Someone over this fault
is constantly shaking my house.

I don't know

I don't know
if they were ugly or beautiful,
sad or cheerful,
in despair or ...

I erased the words.

This nonexistent poem
sounds more like my days.

Each day that passes

Each day that passes
cuts me into pieces.

I gather the pieces,
stick them together,
one piece is missing.

Each day that passes
I get leaner and leaner.

If you ever find those missing parts,
piece them together
and you will see the real me.
The rest is just a senseless puzzle
wherein no one could tell
th player from the plaything.

FROM

TICK TOCK OF YOUR STEPS

My arms are open wide

My arms are open wide
and if you don't jump in,
I would be just a scarecrow.

The scarecrow crossed his arms

The scarecrow crossed his arms,
a bird locked in an embrace!

So many metonymies and metaphors

So many metonymies and metaphors,
so many similes,
yet nothing to resemble you.

I closed my eyes on all;
Everything turned into you.

I was a god once

I was a god once.
I created you.
As soon as I set my eyes on you,
I was ruined.

I was a heavy and dense cloud

I was a heavy and dense cloud,
sad and faraway.
How could I cut the distance short
but to fall drop by drop
down to your cheeks?

When the sky cleared,
a breeze was caressing your cheeks.
It was not my hand.

If there were a door between us

If there were a door between us,
I would knock it on,
I would knock it down.

If there were a wall between us,
I would climb it up, climb it down,
I would crumble it.

If there were a mountain, a sea,
I would step on the world map
and draw a new map.

But there is nothing between us,
nothing.

And with nothing
you can do nothing.

About the Author

Born in 1954, Shahab Mogharabin is an award-winning Iranian poet. After completing his secondary education in his home city of Isfahan, Mogharabin moved to Tehran and entered Sharif University of Technology to study Chemical Engineering, which he later abandoned to pursue his literary ambitions. In 2002, he founded Ahang—e—Digar, an independent poetry publishing company along with two fellow poets, Shams Langeroodi and Hafez Moosavi, where he passionately promoted young and aspiring poets. Since the early 1980s, Mogharabin's poems have appeared in various journals in Iran. He has published eight collections of poetry and two selections in Persian.

Titles of his books include:

Grief of Flights, 1979
Dark and Bright Steps, 1986
Words as Minutes, 1992
By the side of the Purple Road, I Saw My Childhood, 2003; (Winner of Karnameh Poetry Award, 2004)
Selected Poems, 2006
Wind Will Leaf through This Book, 2008
Whistling in the Dark, 2010
Somebody Knocked at the Door, 2013; (Finalist for the Khabarnegaran Poetry Award, 2015)
Tick Tock of Your Steps, 2015
Selected Poems, 2015

9 781947 021426